Alan Bullard

Carols

10 carols for mixed voices

Contents

MUSIC DEPARTMENT

OXFORD

UNIVERSITY PRESS

OXFORD
UNIVERSITY PRESS

Great Clarendon Street, Oxford OX2 6DP, England
198 Madison Avenue, New York, NY 10016, USA

Oxford University Press is a department of the University of Oxford.
It furthers the University's aim of excellence in research, scholarship,
and education by publishing worldwide in

Oxford New York

Auckland Cape Town Hong Kong Karachi
Kuala Lumpur Madrid Melbourne Mexico City Nairobi
New Delhi Shanghai Taipei Toronto

With offices in

Argentina Austria Brazil Chile Czech Republic France Greece
Guatemala Hungary Italy Japan Poland Portugal Singapore
South Korea Switzerland Thailand Turkey Ukraine Vietnam

Oxford is a registered trade mark of Oxford University Press
in the UK and in certain other countries

1 3 5 7 9 10 8 6 4 2

ISBN 978–0–19–336485–1

Music and text origination by
Enigma Music Production Services, Amersham, Bucks.
Printed in Great Britain on acid-free paper by
Halstan & Co. Ltd., Amersham, Bucks.

Cover image reproduced by permission of Alan Bullard

Composer's note

This collection contains ten of the carols I have written over the last decade, ranging from *Angel Alleluias* in 1998 to *This night* in 2009. It includes three brand-new carols, written specially for this collection, as well as a selection of those previously published by OUP, three of which have been newly arranged for SATB choir.

The poems used date from the 15th to 21st centuries. Joy, mystery, wonder, and nostalgia are all to be found in these verses, as we marvel at the strange events, difficult journeys, and persecutions linked to that miraculous birth so many years ago.

Many of these carols tell the traditional Christmas story, though each with a different focus. In *A boy is born in Bethlehem* we rejoice at Jesus's birth, but we also see the wise men gingerly stepping into the stable, not sure what they might find; in *Angel Alleluias* the focus is on the message of the angels, perhaps even playing tambourines as they sing; and in *Hill-side Carol* we are on the bleak and frosty hills with the shepherds, the peacefulness of the night suddenly interrupted by a bright star and a heavenly message, telling of God on earth. *Ring the bells* sings exuberantly and excitedly of the joys of Christmas, whereas *The Gracious Gift* gently pictures Mary rocking Jesus, a New Year gift for all humankind.

Some of these carols are about contrast. *Glory to the Christ Child* brings the 'blessed babe divine' into hushed musical perspective, contrasting with lively syncopated joyfulness; *And all the stars looked down* emphasizes the contrast between the traditional manger scene and the 'real' world outside, aspects that are unified in the last verse as the vision of Christ reaches out to all; and *Star of Wonder* takes the well-known poem and highlights the difference between the long and dangerous journey of the kings and the optimistic and joyful message of the star.

Finally, there are two carols representing two very different traditions. *And can this newborn mystery* presents a thoughtful and vivid poem by a contemporary hymn-writer highlighting the questions that many share today as they grapple with the mystery of 'an infant learning how to feed'; while *This night* takes us to a world far-removed, as the poem's strange blend of Christian and pagan imagery powerfully tells of the long, cold night awaiting Jesus's birth.

I'd like to thank all the choirs who have sung my carols, and the staff at OUP for encouraging me to make this collection and for helping it to come to fruition.

I hope you enjoy it.

Alan Bullard
Winter 2008–9

Index of Orchestrations

Orchestral accompaniments for the following carols are available to hire from the publisher's Hire Library or appropriate agent:

A boy is born in Bethlehem (Puer natus)
2fl, ob, 2cl, bsn(opt), 2hn(IIopt), str

And can this newborn mystery
2fl, ob, 2cl, bsn, 2hn, timp(opt), str

Hill-side Carol
fl or treble recorder solo, ob(opt), 2cl(opt), bsn(opt), 2hn(opt), glock(opt), hp(opt), str

Ring the bells
2fl, ob(opt), 2cl, bsn(opt), 2hn, tpt, 2tbn(opt), glock(opt), hp/pno(opt), str

Star of Wonder
2fl(IIopt), ob(opt), 2cl, bsn(opt), 2hn, 2tpt(IIopt), 2tbn(opt), btbn(opt), tuba(opt), timp(opt), perc(opt), str

This night
2fl, ob(opt), 2cl, bsn(opt), 2hn, tpt(opt), 2tbn(opt), btbn(opt), tuba(opt), timp/perc(opt), hp(opt), str

A boy is born in Bethlehem
(Puer natus)

Latin text from *Piae Cantiones*, 1582
English translation from
The New Oxford Book of Carols (adapted AB)

ALAN BULLARD
(b. 1947)

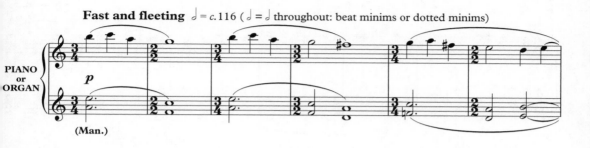

Also available separately in an arrangement for upper voices with optional baritone part (ISBN 978–0–19–335641–2).

sing, all Je - ru - sa - lem,_____ Al - le - lu - ia, al - le -
gau - det   Ie - ru - sa - lem,_____   Al - le - lu - ia,   al - le -

- lu - - ia!_____   The
- *lu - - ia!_____   Cog -*

ox   and   ass   that   Child   a - dored,   Al - le - lu - ia,   And
- no - vit   bos   et   a - si - nus,   Al - le - lu - ia,   Quod

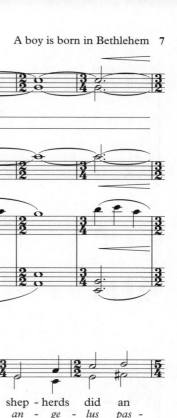

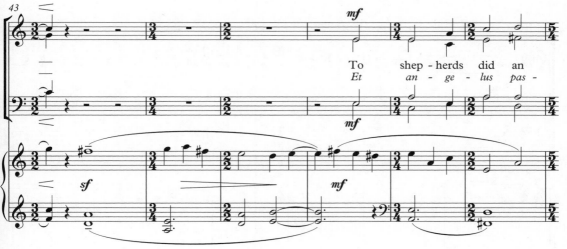

knew he was their heav'n - ly Lord.
pu - er e - rat Do - mi - nus.

To shep - herds did an
Et an - ge - lus pas -

an - gel come, Al - le - lu - ia,_____ al - le -
-to - ri - bus, Al - le - lu - ia, al - le -

(Piano: 8va----

-lu – ia,   To_ tell them that there was_ born a

-lu – ia,   Re – ve – lat quis sit_ Do – mi-

(8)

(Ped.)

Son,____ Al – le – lu – ia,   al – le – lu – – ia!

- nus,____ Al – le – lu – ia,   al – le lu – ia!

(Man.)

T.
B.

The   wise men came from dis – tant

Ma – gi de lon – ge ve – ni-

Al – le – lu – ia,_____ al – le – lu – ia, To__
Al – le – lu – ia,_____ al – le – lu – ia, Na-

give__ the gifts to the new – born Son,_____ Al – le –
-tum sa – lu – tant ho – mi – nem,_____ Al – le –

-lu – ia, al – le – lu – – ia!_____ At
-lu – ia, al – le – lu – – ia!_____ In

(Ped.)

(Organ: LH/pedal 8ve higher until end)

And all the stars looked down

Gilbert Keith Chesterton
(1874–1936)

ALAN BULLARD
(b. 1947)

This carol may be transposed up a semitone into E flat minor.

First published in *The Ivy and the Holly: 14 contemporary carols* (ISBN 978–0–19–336180–5).

December 2007

And can this newborn mystery

Brian Wren
(b. 1936)

ALAN BULLARD
(b. 1947)

This carol is based on the hymn-tune 'High Leigh', written by the composer for the above words.

(**Piano**: omit upper small notes)
(**Organ**: omit lower small notes)

Angel Alleluias

15th century (modernized and adapted AB)

ALAN BULLARD
(b. 1947)

*The optional percussion part may be performed on any appropriate instrument, such as maracas or tambourine, or clapped.

Also available separately (ISBN 978-0-19-343242-0).

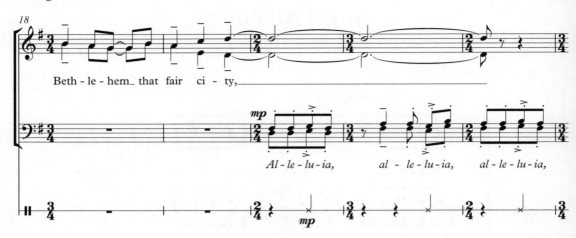

Beth - le - hem_ that fair ci - ty,_____

Al - le - lu - ia, al - le - lu - ia, al - le - lu - ia,

al - le - lu, An - gels sung there_____ with_ mirth and glee:_

Al - le - lu - ia, al - le - lu - ia, al - le - lu - ia, al - le - lu - ia. Al - le - lu - ia,

al - le - lu - ia, al - le - lu - ia, al - le - lu._____

mf legato

Some shep - herds saw_ those

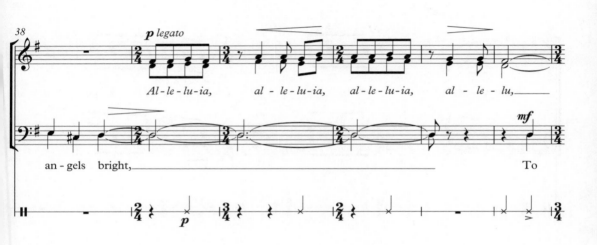

p legato

Al - le - lu - ia, al - le - lu - ia, al - le - lu - ia, al - le - lu,_____

an - gels bright,_____ To

mf

p

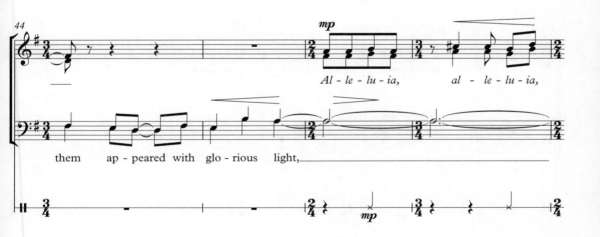

mp

Al - le - lu - ia, al - le - lu - ia,

them ap - peared with glo - rious light,_____

mp

al - le - lu - ia, al - le - lu, And said: 'God's Son is

born to - night!' Al - le - lu - ia, al - le - lu - ia, al - le - lu - ia, al - le-

-lu - ia. Al - le - lu - ia, al - le - lu - ia, al - le - lu - ia, al - le - lu, This

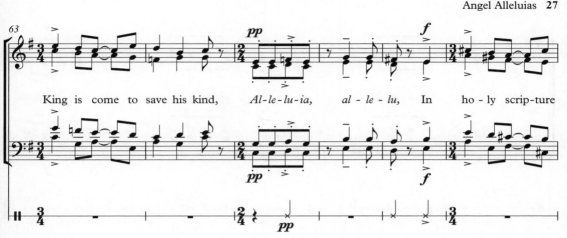

King is come to save his kind, _Al-le-lu-ia,_ _al - le - lu,_ In ho - ly scrip-ture

as we find, _Al-le-lu-ia,_ _al - le-lu,_ There-fore this song_____ we____

have in mind:___ _Al - le-lu-ia,_ _al - le-lu-ia,_ _al - le-lu-ia,_ _al - le-_

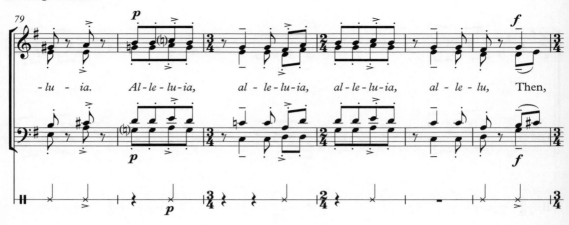

-lu - ia. Al - le - lu - ia, al - le - lu - ia, al - le - lu - ia, al - le - lu, Then,

dear - est Lord, for thy great grace,_____

Al - le - lu - ia, al - le - lu - ia, al - le - lu - ia,

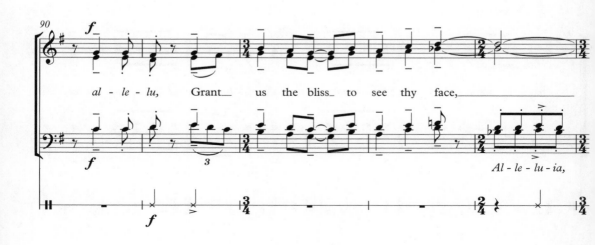

al - le - lu, Grant__ us the bliss__ to see thy face,_____

Al - le - lu - ia,

al - le - lu, Where we may

al - le - lu - ia, al - le - lu - ia,

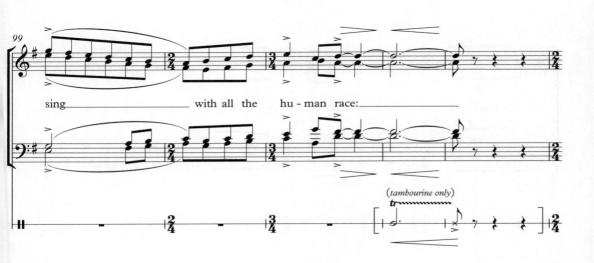

sing_____ with all the hu - man race:

(tambourine only)

(strict tempo to end)

Al - le - lu - ia, al - le - lu - ia, al - le - lu - ia, al - le - lu - ia.

Al - le - lu - ia, al - le - lu - ia, al - le - lu - ia, al - le - lu - ia.

Al - le - lu - ia, al - le - lu - ia, al - le - lu - ia, al - le - lu - ia.

Al - le - lu - ia, al - le - lu - ia, al - le - lu - ia, al - le - lu - ia.

Christmas 1998

Glory to the Christ Child

Verses taken from BM Add. MS 29401 (*c.*1610)

ALAN BULLARD
(b. 1947)

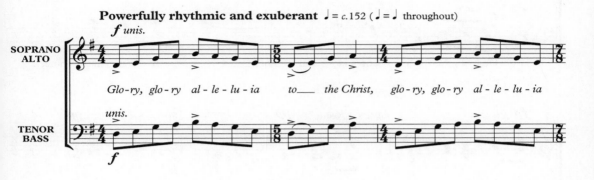

Also available separately (ISBN 978–0–19–335567–5).

Out of the or - ient cry - stal skies A blaz - ing star did shine,

Out of the or - ient cry - stal skies____ A star did shine,

Show - ing the place where sleep - ing lies___ A bless - ed babe di - vine.

Glo - ry, glo - ry al - le - lu - ia to___ the Christ, glo - ry, glo - ry al - le - lu - ia to___ the Christ Child!

Glo - ry, glo - ry al - le - lu - ia to___ the Christ Child, glo - ry al - le - lu - ia to___ the Christ Child!

Al - le - lu - ia! Glo - ry, glo - ry to___ the Christ, al - le - lu - ia!

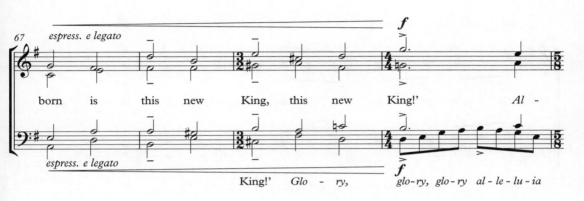

Hill-side Carol

Clive Sansom (1910–81)
(adapted AB)

ALAN BULLARD
(b. 1947)

*Play small notes if flute or treble recorder not available.

Also available separately (ISBN 978-0-19-343253-6). The part for flute or treble recorder is printed on p. 72.

The eve-ning was calm,_____ The air____ so still, Si - lence and rest - ful peace_____

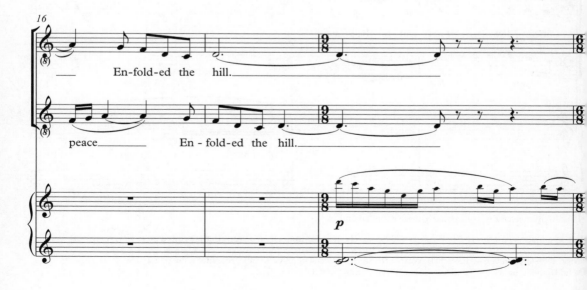

And so we have come,_____ Our

day's work done,_____ Our loves, our hopes, our - selves_____ We give to your

Son._____

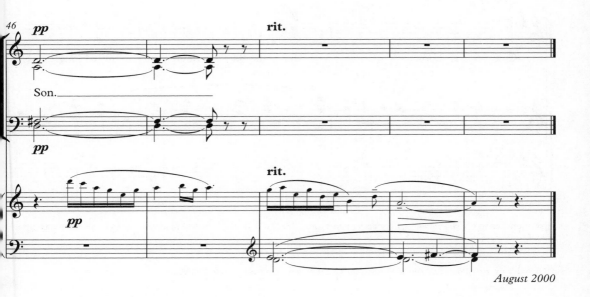

August 2000

Ring the bells

Frances Jane Crosby
(1820–1915)

ALAN BULLARD
(b.1947)

First published in *For Him all Stars: 15 carols for upper voices* (ISBN 978–0–19–335569–9) in an arrangement for three-part upper voices.

Come and hail him with a song.

Wake your harps, ye an-gels bright; Sing a-loud ye

Sing a-loud ye

hosts of light: Sing as on that ho-ly night:

hosts of light: Sing, sing as on that ho-ly

hosts of light: Sing, sing, sing as on that

Star of Wonder

John Henry Hopkins
(1820–91)

ALAN BULLARD
(b. 1947

*Omit small notes if performing on piano.

First published in Bullard (ed.), *The Oxford Book of Flexible Anthems* (ISBN 978–0–19–335895–9) in an arrangement for unison voices, SA, or SA Men.

Hill-side Carol

*Bars 21–8: soprano and alto parts optional

The soprano part may be sung by altos, tenors, and basses in unison from bar 47 until the end, with sopranos singing the descant line.

August 2000

Summer 2007 and Christmas 200

The Gracious Gift

attrib. James, John, and Robert Wedderburn (*c.* 1567)

ALAN BULLARD
(b. 1947)

spreet = spirit

²*glor* = glory
³*richt* = right

Glo - ry to God e - ter - nal - ly, Who gave his on - ly
Glo - ry to God e - ter - nal - ly, Who gave his
Glo - ry to God e - ter - nal - ly, Who gave his
Glo - ry to God e - ter - nal - ly, Who gave his on - ly

Son for me, The an - gels' joys for us to
Son for me, The an - gels' joys for to
Son for me, The an - gels' joys for us to

hear, The gra - cious gift, the gra - cious gift, The

gra - cious gift
gra - cious, gra - cious gift of this New Year.
gra - cious gift

meno mosso e rit.

December 2008

This night

Trad. Hebridean

ALAN BULLARD
(b. 1947)

*The first note of the accompaniment may be omitted.

(Piano: *Ped.* ___

_is born Je - sus,_____ Son___ of the King of Glo - ry,_

_is born___ Je - sus,_____ Son___ of the King of Glo - ry,_

night is born Je - sus,_____ Glo - ry al - le - lu -

night is born_____ Je - sus,_ Glo - ry al - le - lu -

(Man.)

calming down   **poco rit.**

This night_____ is born to us the root_____ of___ our

This night_____ born to us the root_____ of___ our

- ia, Glo - ry al - le - lu - ia, al - le - lu - ia,

- ia, Glo - ry al - le - lu - ia, al - le - lu - ia,

calming down   **poco rit.**

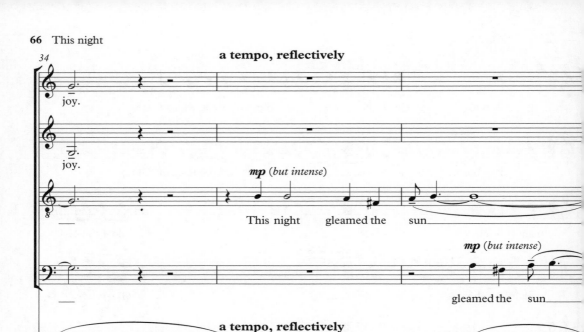

Christ the King of great - ness, Christ____ the King of glo - ry is come, is__ come. is come,____ Al - le - lu - ia,____ al-le-lu - ia, al-le-lu - ia,____

poco rit. **Meno mosso** ♩ = c.48 Al-le - lu - ia, Glo - ri - a,____ al-le-lu - ia,

(Man.)

SOLO or TUTTI TENORS
This night   is the   long   night,_____

al-le-lu - ia,

Tempo I, simply and expressively

lunga   *p*

Glowed to him   wood___ and   tree,_____

lunga (TUTTI)

lunga

Tempo I, simply and expressively

lunga

mp

Glowed to him   mount___ and   sea,

mount___ and   sea,

mount___ and   sea,_____

mp

Glowed to him land___ and plain,___

When that his foot___ was come to

earth.___

(Piano: *Ped.*)
(Organ: Ped. 32', 16')

Flute (or Treble Recorder)

Hill-side Carol

ALAN BULLARD
(b. 1947)

This page may be enlarged on a photocopier as required.